DECOMPRESSED

Gratitude, Reflections, and Breath Prayers
for Healing and Thriving

ALISON WAKELEE

Decompressed
©2023 Alison Wakelee

All rights reserved. This book or any portion thereof may not be reproduced or used in any manner whatsoever without the express written permission of the publisher except for the use of brief quotations in a book review.

ISBN: 978-1-66789-014-2

CONTENTS

Introduction	1
Lesson One: Believe in Miracles	7
Lesson Two: The Power of Affirmative Prayer	9
Lesson Three: The Suddenly Moment	11
Lesson Four: Grateful Tank Top	14
Lesson Five: My First Sick Day	16
Lesson Six: Go a Little Further Each Day	18
Lesson Seven: Misery Is a Choice	20
Lesson Eight: The Blessing of Family	22
Lesson Nine: Cry for a Day and Move On	24
Lesson Ten: The Only Way Out Is Through	26
Lesson Eleven: Praying for Others	29
Lesson Twelve: Flowers	31
Lesson Thirteen: A Stupid Thing to Do	34
Lesson Fourteen: Integrity	36
Lesson Fifteen: Walking to Work	39
Lesson Sixteen: Surrender	41
Lesson Seventeen: Angel in the Woods	43

Lesson Eighteen: Blessed with Friends	46
Lesson Nineteen: The Lesson of Ivana Trump	48
Lesson Twenty: The Hardware Store Angel	51
Lesson Twenty-One: Delay Does Not Mean Denial	53
Lesson Twenty-Two: Message in the Rocks	56
Lesson Twenty-Three: Shannon's Blog	58
Lesson Twenty-Four: Spirit Animal Clementine	60
Lesson Twenty-Five: They Had Little, Yet Were Generous With Me	62
Lesson Twenty-Six: Ripple Effect	64
Lesson Twenty-Seven: God Never Blinks	66
Lesson Twenty-Eight: Twenty-Twenty-Twenty-Four Hours to Go!	68
Lesson Twenty-Nine: Healed	70
Lesson Thirty: Grateful for the Journey	73

INTRODUCTION

Life is full of peaks and valleys. Literally. In late June 2022, I had just returned from an amazing trip to Machu Picchu, Peru, where I had hiked to some of the most gorgeous mountain peaks, looking down at the wonder of the earth. Llamas filled the path that was made up of long stretches of dry terrain mixed with steep, natural steps. The whole trip was such a dream come true. With each step, the trail became more beautiful, colorful, and vibrant than the next. I was smiling from ear to ear at my fortune to see such beauty, and that I got to experience it with one of my best friends, my lifelong friend, Shannon.

The day after I returned from Peru was just a normal day. I went to work at Eaton Corporation, where I have a job that I love in Information Technology (IT). The day flew by, catching up on e-mails, telling coworkers about how amazing Peru was, and spending time in meetings. When I got home from work, I just wanted to get to OrangeTheory, a fitness studio focusing on high-intensity interval training, that I had gone to for years and was just around the corner from my house. I couldn't wait to see my fitness friends and to sweat! Being a creature of habit, I was elated to get back into routine after being on vacation. I was excited by the thought of running on the treadmill, rowing, and lifting weights that night. I had been looking forward to it all day.

I got home from work and was unpacking my suitcase and finishing putting away my laundry when I realized that I was running a bit behind schedule and needed to change and get ready to head to my workout. I hurriedly threw off the new pale blue dress I wore to work that day, took out my rose gold hoop earrings, and slipped on my sports bra, heart rate monitor, tank top with the word Grateful across the chest, running pants, and socks. It all seemed so normal. With my phone in one hand and my keys in the other, I quickly skipped down the steps of my townhouse, where I lived alone. I made my way down one flight of stairs and a small carpeted landing before making the turn to the second flight. On the first stair, I knew something felt off. My sock had slipped on the carpet and I was falling. Falling straight back.

No! Please no! I thought as I skidded down the stairs, straight on my back, each stair hitting me with a thud as I fell all the way down. Finally coming to a stop, I noticed my head was on the last step and my body was on the cold tile landing of my floor. I was out of breath. The pain on the right-hand side of my back was crippling. My vision was becoming tunnel-like. *Don't pass out. You're okay. You're going to be okay. Don't pass out,* became my mantra as I lay there, writhing in pain. *You're going to be okay. You're okay,* I thought to myself over and over again. My back was throbbing. Waves of pain kept coming. On top of it, I couldn't catch my breath. I knew immediately something was wrong. *Is my spinal fusion okay?* I wondered. I had had a spinal fusion in 1999 to correct an advanced case of scoliosis and had eighteen-inch rods down my spine. *Could the rods have come loose? That's impossible, right? You're okay. You're going to be okay. Don't pass out.*

Maybe just being stunned from the fall knocked the wind out of me, I thought. *Maybe I can still get up, walk it off, and make it to OrangeTheory in time.* I tried again to lift myself up and move, but I simply couldn't. The pain was too much. After ten minutes of lying in pain, struggling to catch my breath, I knew I wasn't making it to OrangeTheory, or anywhere else, that night. I knew something was wrong, and I'd better get it checked out as quickly as I could.

Knowing that I absolutely needed to, I mustered up enough strength to push myself on to my hands and knees. Making it there, I screamed out in agony, trying to steady myself in the new position. Trying not to collapse under the pain, I crawled around, finally finding my phone on the second-to-the-last stair, which was clutched in my hand at the start of the way down the stairs, but had quickly been lost when I started to fall. I knew this was more than I could handle on my own. I needed to call for help. I needed to get to the hospital as soon as possible. I was able to pick up the phone and dial. "I think I'm hurt. I need to get to the emergency room," I said weakly between tears and shortness of breath.

The next few minutes of making it to the hospital were a blur. As I arrived in the emergency room at Ahuja Medical Center in Beachwood, Ohio, just more than a mile from my house, I tried to put on my bravest front, but couldn't hold back the tears that were streaming down my face. I explained to the doctors what had happened and how I was scared that I wasn't able to catch my breath. The emergency room was busy, so they had me wait in a small room while they lined up the tests I needed to go through. I frantically rummaged around in my wallet to find my health insurance card and started filling out medical history forms.

I went from x-rays to CT scans to blood pressure checks to getting an IV put in. I was able to call my family and let them know that I had fallen and was in the hospital. My mom and sister who lived a bit less than an hour away from, came to the emergency room to comfort me and to hold my hand while I awaited the test results. I could see the concern in their eyes. The only place I felt comfortable was standing next to the gurney, bent over, with my hands on the mattress and my head hanging. Finally, the doctor came in to talk to me about my injuries.

I was fully expecting him to say, "You're okay. You'll be sore and bruised for a few days. Take some ibuprofen and rest, and you'll be better by the weekend and running again at OrangeTheory by this time next week."

That's not what happened.

"You have several serious injuries," the doctor began. "You have broken your neck. You have a compression fracture in your C7 vertebrae. A compression fracture is where your vertebrae gets compressed—or squished—and shifts the alignment with the rest of your vertebrae. Additionally, your eleventh rib is broken and has punctured your right lung, which has partially deflated. You also have fractured the L1 vertebrae in your lower spine, and the tip has broken off. We need to immobilize you immediately."

I was shocked. I knew I was hurt, but had no idea that all these things had happened in my body. I was immediately put in a stiff and heavy neck brace and told that it was very important that I didn't move my head at all. The shock of the news caught up with me, and I grabbed my mom's hand as I laid back on the gurney and began to cry all over again.

"How is this possible? I can't believe this happened," I lamented to my mom and sister. They both sympathetically squeezed my hands and wiped the tears from my cheeks with a tissue. Little did I know that the neck brace would stay on me for the next seventy days, twenty-four hours a day. At that point, lying there in the emergency room, I couldn't see how the pieces would fit together or the purpose in what I was going through. I also didn't know the many lessons I would learn, the many experiences I would have, and the many ways I would see God show up in my life over and over again during these days. What were the hardest days of my life, in many ways, also turned out to be areas where my biggest blessings turned up. This is my story of becoming *decompressed* – thirty lessons that I learned over my seventy days of healing.

LESSON ONE:
Believe in Miracles

"Had your vertebrae pushed one millimeter further, you would have been paralyzed from the neck down," the trauma-ward doctor told me as he secured the second brace around my neck, tightening it, making sure my ability to move my neck in any way was now completely gone. My eyes filled with tears and blurred with that news.

One millimeter. I could have been paralyzed? Me? Paralyzed? One millimeter. I remember doing an Internet search of how big one millimeter was a few days later, and finding it was less than a credit card's width. I couldn't even grasp that reality in my head. I was always incredibly active. *Just the day before the fall, I had returned from hiking the Inca Trail in Machu Picchu, Peru, up and down narrow and steep natural steps without getting a scratch on me, and today I could have been paralyzed from falling down my own staircase at home?* After the initial shock of the news came, suddenly another feeling bubbled up inside. I had a deep feeling that I had just been a part of a miracle. Although I was frustrated, scared, and horrified at the extent of my injuries, deep down I knew that it could have been worse. So much worse. I had a deep awareness that God must have been with me when I fell, protecting me. Stopping the vertebrae just in time to ensure I'd have a favorable outcome. Ensuring the spinal fusion that I had when I was just fourteen years old was still intact and unharmed. Watching over me and showing me His love in the very moment when I was the weakest.

You hear about these things happening, but until it happens to you, you don't realize the blessing that it truly is. I'm grateful for that. I'm grateful that in the midst of all of the uncertainty, I witnessed a miracle. I'm grateful that I'll never again take one minute of walking and moving freely for granted. I'm grateful that, in that moment, I realized that being alive and having the ability to do all the things we do on a daily basis is in itself a miracle. I admit that, pretty much every day before then, I never really thought about my ability to move. I just moved. I took for granted that being able to walk and run and climb Machu Picchu was such an honor and a privilege. Miracles happen every day, big and small. Be open to receiving them in unexpected situations and unexpected ways.

Dear God,

Thank you for blessing us each with miracles every day. From each breath that we take to each step that we take, being alive in and of itself is a miracle. Please do not let me take this for granted again. Please open my eyes to seeing the good in every situation and recognizing your healing hand that is always with me.

Amen.

LESSON TWO:
The Power of Affirmative Prayer

The night that I fell, I stayed in the emergency room at Ahuja Medical Center in Beachwood, Ohio, as I awaited the ambulance that would take me to the trauma center downtown for further evaluation and surgical consults. My mom and sister were asked to leave so I could get some rest. I admit it: I was scared. I was hungry. I was tired. I was thirsty. I was wondering if I would need surgery. I was worried about missing work the next day. My mind was flooded with thoughts of *what ifs* and *what will happen next?* I tried to get some rest, but the beeping of machines, the talking of the nurses in the hallway, and the bright lights that streamed in from the happenings in the ER made it difficult to feel relaxed. I lay there in the hospital bed, immobile. I didn't know what else to do, so I began to pray affirmative prayers.

I prayed for what I wanted. I prayed that I would be completely healed from my injuries. I prayed that the pain would become manageable and dissipate completely. I thanked God for his healing hand already being on me. I prayed in assurance that I was going to be okay and that the doctors would give me the best direction and care that would lead to my full recovery. At the end, I affirmed that these prayers had been heard and that healing was already in motion. And, as I discovered over the next seventy days, that is exactly what happened.

The lesson I learned? Ask God for what you want. Affirm that what you are seeking is already happening. Thank God for his provision and that healing and health are already yours. For if you have faith as small as a mustard seed, it will be so.

Dear God,

Thank you for your gift of prayer. Thank you that we can talk to you any time that we need. Thank you for giving us the faith that you are for us and not against us. Thank you for taking good care of us as we heal from the ups and downs of life's journeys. Thank you for listening. Thank you for acting.

Amen.

LESSON THREE:
The Suddenly Moment

The ambulance arrived that would transport me from Ahuja Medical Center to University Hospital of Cleveland's Trauma Center in downtown Cleveland. On the trip, I was strapped to the gurney to keep my spine and neck as stable as possible. My neck brace was on and tight around my neck. We made the thirteen-mile, bumpy drive and arrived at the hospital. In the trauma unit, the medical teams were kind, but strict. They told me absolutely not to move even my fingers or hands, that it was crucial that I stay as still as possible to ensure my injuries didn't progress. As they asked me endless questions about my medical history, I couldn't help but try to nod a bit when a statement they made was valid or to shake my head just slightly when it wasn't. They reminded me again that movement could result in paralysis and asked me again to stay as still as I possibly could. I laid on the gurney, totally immobile, for hour after hour. *Is this going to be the rest of my life?* I wondered. Every ten minutes or so, a nurse would pop in to check my vital signs and to ensure that I wasn't moving.

"You're going to be in here a very long time, I'm afraid," the nurse explained when I asked if she thought I would be able to go home that day. "My guess is a minimum of a few days, most likely a couple of weeks."

Panic set in. I was supposed to start a new position at work that day. It was my dream job. I had just been offered the promotion and accepted it with such excitement, and I was eager to start. Now I'd have to miss a couple of weeks? I was terrified. My mind was swirling with so many questions that were yet to be answered. I was wheeled back and forth to different x-rays, a catheter was inserted so I didn't have to move to go pee, and I started to wonder if the nurse was right. Maybe I would be here for a very long time.

After lying around for several hours, staring at the ceiling, a doctor popped in.

"Good news. I've reviewed all of your x-rays, CT scans, and medical history. Your neck looks stable. It's serious, but stable. You will have to remain in the brace at all times, but our team determined you will not need surgery at this point. Immobilization should heal it over time. You may have noticed that it's a big easier to breathe. Your lung reinflated on its own, which is really good, so there's no need for any additional treatment there. Your rib and L1 vertebrae that are broken will be painful, but will heal on their own in a few weeks. I'm going to start your discharge papers so you can continue to recover at home. Remember, you must keep the neck brace on at all times, but you can sit up if you'd like and walk around the room a bit."

I was absolutely stunned. How did we go from 'you may be immobile on your back for weeks' to being discharged? A big smile came across my face. I was in utter disbelief. The doctor helped undo the straps that held my body rigidly to the gurney to keep me from moving and pushed the button to raise my bed. Just sitting up felt life changing after nearly twenty hours of laying flat.

The big change made me think of the word suddenly. Suddenly, my situation changed. Did you know that the word *suddenly* appears in the Bible eighty-seven times? Eighty-seven! Suddenly, situations change for the better. Suddenly, something good that they didn't see coming happened. And I just had a suddenly moment of my own! Suddenly, I was able to get ready to go home. Suddenly, I could walk around again. Suddenly, I could see life returning to somewhat normal more quickly than I'd anticipated. Suddenly, I was filled with hope again.

Do you ever have moments that you don't see how they could ever turn around? The evidence seems stacked that the situation is going to remain for a very long time. Our God is a God of suddenlies.

Dear God,

Thank you for the suddenly moments in our lives. May we never double that, even in our darkest hours, suddenly you can step in and everything can change in an instant. Thank you for suddenly turning my situation around.

Amen.

LESSON FOUR:
Grateful Tank Top

When I had fallen down my stairs, I had to smile at what I was wearing at the time. It was a black tank top with the word "Grateful" across the chest in white lettering. The irony. I had forgotten I was wearing it until the doctor finally let me stand up and go to the bathroom in the trauma unit while he prepared my discharge papers. I caught a glimpse of myself in the mirror. The make-up that I had applied the morning of the fall was mostly worn off. My mascara was in black streaks down my face. My hair was limp and frizzed from lying on the bed, immobile for the past twenty hours. My neck was in a stiff brace that was tight and rigid. *Grateful.* I smirked at my pathetic reflection in the mirror. *How could I be grateful when I was bruised and broken? How could I be grateful when I was in agonizing pain? How could I be grateful when the world as I knew it just minutes before the fall would be on hold for the next couple of months, maybe forever?*

But catching a glimpse of myself in the mirror, I had to giggle at myself. And in that moment, a new perspective came over me. Although I was feeling at an all-time low at the time, I realized I truly was grateful. I was grateful that my sister and mom had rushed to meet me at the hospital and to be there with me. I was grateful that although I had a long recovery ahead of me, I was standing. I was able to walk to the bathroom on my own. I was grateful that I would soon be able to go home and rest in my own bed. I was grateful to be alive and on the road to recovery.

How many times have we overlooked the long list of things to be grateful for because we were blinded by our own pain? How many things in your life now can you list that you're grateful for in this very moment? Be grateful. It opens us up to see all the good, no matter what our current circumstances are.

Dear God,

I am grateful for the blessings, big and small, that surround me at all times. Help me resist the temptation to be negative and succumb to feelings of sadness and self-pity. Thank you for showing us that we can be grateful in all circumstances, when our eyes are fixed on You.

Amen.

LESSON FIVE:

My First Sick Day

I had been working in IT at Eaton Corporation for nearly nine years without taking a single sick day. I held that as a badge of honor. I prided myself on being in good physical and emotional health and working through days where I wasn't feeling 100 percent. My pride kept me from admitting there were days when I could have benefited from resting and relaxing. I wanted to appear like the perfect employee. Then, this fall happened.

As I lay in the hospital bed, I even wondered if my mom could bring my laptop to the hospital so I could log in and attend the meetings that I was supposed to be in that day. I wondered if I could take the meetings that I needed to take and I wouldn't have to admit to anyone that I had fallen and gotten injured.

Then it hit me: *Why? Why was I afraid of admitting I was sick or injured? Why was I embarrassed that I wasn't the perfect employee?* I would never have judged anyone for taking time off of work to recover from an injury, so why didn't I have the grace to hold that same compassion for myself? That realization made me stop in my tracks. My worth wasn't based on being in a perfect state. I needed to learn this lesson. I texted my boss and let her know what happened and that I wouldn't be in. She immediately responded with love, empathy, and compassion. I gave myself permission to rest, recover, and unplug from work—and my healing began. Not only healing from my fall but also healing my warped idea that I needed to be perfect at all times. I needed to let go of the fear that perfectionism was cleverly disguised in. I needed to give myself the grace that I would give others. And in that moment, I did. And it felt good. Really, really good.

Dear God,

Thank you for helping me realize that I don't have to be perfect. Forgive me for the times that I put my self-worth in the idea of perfectionism. Thank you for showing me that I am human. Thank you for humbling me. Thank you for showing me that my worth comes from you, not other's perceptions of me. This is a lesson I needed to learn.

Amen.

LESSON SIX:
Go a Little Further Each Day

Before the fall, I was a walker. I loved walking endlessly around my neighborhood, local metro parks, or even, on rainy days, laps around my house. I got positive reinforcement from my Apple Watch, which sent me motivating messages when I reached my move goal each day. The day after I got home from the hospital, I felt stiff and tense and didn't feel like walking at all. I felt like curling up in a ball and dying, to be honest. That day, I went home, I fell asleep, and didn't even put on my Apple Watch, knowing that I was perfectly content to lay around and that my body needed rest more than anything else. But, I made up my mind, the next day, I would try to take a short walk. I live in a condo, near the back of the complex, and the mailboxes are out by the road. While it is just more than one-tenth of a mile to the mailbox and back, it seemed like a journey. That day, with my sister walking slowly next to me, I reached my first small victory by walking to the mailbox and back. As soon as I got back in my condo and walked painstakingly slowly up my stairs, it was time for me to lie down again and rest. Two days earlier, it would have been absurd to me that walking such a short distance would tire me out at all. But that day, it felt like an epic achievement. The next day, I thought, *I'll try to do that twice.* I went from walking back and forth to my mailbox twice to walking one mile to two miles. Eighteen days after the fall, I walked a whopping twelve miles! How did I do it? By going a little further each day. By affirming under my breath, "I can do all things through Christ who strengthens me." I had the will do overcome and get better, with God's help, one step at a time.

Dear God,

Thank you for giving me the perseverance to want to get better, day-by-day. Thank you for guiding my feet to step carefully and safely each moment of the day. Thank you for the ability to simply walk—to see the beauty of the summer.

Amen.

LESSON SEVEN:

Misery Is a Choice

Not wanting me to stay alone, even when I resisted, my sister picked me up one day and took me to my parents' house to spend the Fourth of July weekend. I didn't feel like going. I like my house. I like to have my things. I like to sleep in my bed. But, I knew that with my injuries, it was hard for me to sit up on my own when I was lying down. I wasn't allowed to lift more than five pounds. I was still groggy from the pain medicine that they had given me at the hospital, so I finally agreed that it was probably a good option to stay with my parents the first few days of my recovery.

To pass the time, my parents, sister, and I decided to pull out some old games that we hadn't played since my childhood. There was one game in particular that my grandma had at her house, a board game that took place in a haunted house. It was so silly, yet entertaining. We started the night off with that one. We all had to roll our eyes at the ridiculousness of the game—from falling into the bat cave to being scared by a ghost and losing your turn, we made our way through the game, and memories flooded back of how we would make Grandma play that endlessly when we had slept over at her house.

Next up was the game *Ransom Notes*, a fun word game that we had never tried before, one my sister had just bought. As we played, we all started to laugh so hard. Although my back was incredibly painful, I held it with one hand as I belly laughed at the game. At the end of the night, I realized that misery is a choice. I could have stayed home by myself, feeling sorry for myself, and noticing my pain. Thankfully, I went to my parent's house where we played goofy games and laughed the night away. Not once that night did I think *Poor me*. Instead, I was thinking how sweet life was that, although I was hurt, I was alive, surrounded my family, and laughing nonstop. Misery is choice. Joy is a choice. Choose joy.

Dear God,

Thank you for allowing me to see that there is always a choice in life between misery and joy. Thank you for showing me so clearly that joy is always the right choice.

Amen.

LESSON EIGHT:
The Blessing of Family

I've been blessed with a wonderful, caring, and loving family. Although we don't always see eye-to-eye, I know that my family will be there for me in a minute, no questions asked, whenever I need them. When I arrived at the emergency room the night of my fall, my mom was the first one I called. She told me she loved me and that she'd be there as soon as she could drive there and that she would be praying for me. The second person that I called was my sister. She, too, immediately left work to drive to the ER to be by my side. My mom and sister stayed with me throughout the evening, as test results and diagnoses came trickling in. They held my hand. They assured me that everything was going to be okay. They lovingly stroked my forehead and hair and they let me know they'd be there for me throughout the entirety of my healing.

For the next seventy days, they kept that promise. From staying with me at home the night after my fall, to driving me to their house to take care of me for several days after my fall, to driving to my house to take me grocery shopping, to hair and nail appointments (A girl's gotta look her best!), to helping me clean around my house, they were there for me every step of the way. I could call my mom, night or day, to talk through how I was feeling—to celebrate on good days and to cry over the phone with on hard days. What an amazing blessing this was. I had always had their support, but the fall highlighted it. They were unwaveringly there for me throughout it all. I'm so grateful for this gift that God has given me and I'm grateful that he opened my eyes to appreciate them even more throughout this experience.

Dear God,

Thank you for the gift of family. Thank you that you hand-picked the souls that would be my parents and sister and placed them in my life. Thank you for the times that they challenge me to see things from different perspectives. Thank you for the laughs and cries along the way. But most of all, thank you that I have a support system that is there for me, without question, day in and day out.

Amen.

LESSON NINE:

Cry for a Day and Move On

Seventy days in a neck brace wasn't all bad, but some days it was incredibly hard. I missed going to the gym. I missed the freedom of driving to wherever I wanted to go anytime I wanted to go. I hated cancelling plans because I couldn't drive to where I needed to be. About a week into this process, I had a day where I cried. I cried for the sudden change thrust upon my life. I cried for the fear of what had happened. I cried for making a mistake and not holding on to the handrail the day I fell, replaying in my head that this was a preventable injury. I cried knowing that I still had several weeks to go, in the heat of the summer, wearing the bulky neck brace. I cried for the pain of my broken rib that was a throbbing, annoying, deep pain in my side. I just cried. The entire day, I let it come in waves. I would cry and then clear up for a bit, and then cry and cry again.

At the end of the day, I told myself, *Okay, you've cried. You've grieved. You can cry again, but for now, you need you to move on.* I prayed for God's help in overcoming the disappointment and fear of it all. I prayed to feel better. I reasoned with God that I wasn't used to feeling bad. I was used to feeling healthy and bubbly, and now I felt just the opposite. I went to bed with tears in my eyes and a stuffy nose from the gentle sobbing I had done all day long, and then I let go. The next morning I woke up. The first thing I noticed is that I was comfortable. I felt warm and cozy in my bed. The next thing that I noticed is that it was bright outside. I had slept the entire night soundly. Then I noticed, I was completely pain free. I smiled. Somewhat in disbelief, I brought my hand to my side where my rib had been hurting so badly the night before. The pain was gone. The pressure was gone. I felt like new. My river of tears the day before had been healing. It had been a release of all the pent-up emotions that I felt since the injury. And when I gave myself space to let it go, the pain, too, left—and never returned. Starting that day, one week after my injuries occurred, my recovery was completely pain free. Not even a trace of the pain remained, or ever returned.

Dear God,

Thank you for the gift of tears. Our tears prove that we are human. They prove that we have emotion. Let us never be too proud to have a good cry. It is healing. It is rejuvenating. It is the river of life that sweeps away sorrow that is replaced with joy in the morning.

Amen.

LESSON TEN:
The Only Way Out Is Through

Before the accident, I had always been a good sleeper. Usually I would lie down and within five minutes drift off into sleep and stay asleep most of the night until morning. If I were to wake up, it was easy for me to turn the pillow to the cool side, readjust, and fall right back asleep.

After the accident, that changed.

The night after I came home from the hospital, I showered, changed into my pajamas, and lay down, just like I normally would. I was used to sleeping on my side, but since I had to keep the neck brace on at all times, I had to lay flat on my back. The tightness of the neck brace felt like a tight hand around my neck at first. Finally getting comfortable, I started to close my eyes and, right before I drifted off, I had a strong feeling of fear come over me. I was worried that if I fell asleep, I would never wake up again. My eyes shot open, my breathing became rapid, my hand immediately reached to the neck brace, trying to loosen its grip from my neck, and I could feel my eyes burn with tears. *You're okay. You're safe. God has you in the palm of his hand. You're okay. You're not going to die. You can sleep,* I told myself, wiping the tears away. A few minutes after that, I believed what I told myself and drifted off into a restful sleep.

The next night, like clockwork, it happened again. Same routine. I'd tell myself that this was just fear talking, that I was safe, that God was protecting me, wipe my tears away, and fall back to sleep.

This happened to me night after night after night for about three weeks straight.

Finally, I told my mom and a couple of friends that this was happening to me. I was embarrassed. I felt weak. I felt unappreciative of how well my recovery was going. My fear seemed completely unjustified and senseless. They listened to me compassionately and told me that it was the trauma being worked out of my system. They assured me not to fight it but to let it be and to keep affirming that I was safe.

That night, it happened again, but it felt less severe. Perhaps getting it out into the open and not holding it inside of me took away some of the power of the fear. The shame around it was gone. It was no longer a secret that I was guarding tightly. The following night, again, but it lessened. By the end of that week, that was no longer happening, and I easily fell asleep in peace and stayed in peace all night.

Trauma has an interesting way of bubbling up and presenting itself. I loved the sage wisdom of my friends: "Don't fight it. The only way out of it is through it." I had to let the pain, the fear, and the uncertainty out in order to get through it. Had I bottled it up or not allowed it to come, it may have kept coming, even now. In times of discomfort, how temping is it to try to bypass this step? To drug it, to fight it, to hide it, to feel shame about it. What I learned is that when you acknowledge it and let it pass, that's exactly what happens: It passes. The only way out is through.

Dear God,

Thank you for this important lesson that feeling each feeling is important and valuable, that trying to leapfrog this important step is really short-circuiting the process. Thank you for safely getting me through each step.

Amen.

LESSON ELEVEN:

Praying for Others

Before my fall, my days were typically jam-packed from 5:00 a.m., when I'd wake up for work, until 10:00 p.m., when I'd start preparing to go to bed. From working full-time, to teaching yoga, to going to the gym, to meeting up with friends, to hiking, to being on the board for a local non-for-profit, to volunteering at my church, I had a lot going on. I prided myself on fitting in as much as I could each day. When I suddenly couldn't drive for seventy days as a result of wearing the neck brace, I found myself in the unfamiliar territory of having down time. I tried to watch television. After five minutes, I got bored. I tried to cook new recipes. I'd cook, that would take an hour, and then I'd be back to wondering what I was going to do next. One day, I listened to a sermon online by Joel Osteen about the power of praying for others. It was like a light went off in my head. I could use my time to pray for others!

I made a list of family, friends, and people that were easy to love, and a list of those who were hard to love. Each day, I sat upstairs in my prayer nook and prayed for each of these people. I prayed for their health, happiness, and success. I prayed that their eyes would be opened to seeing Jesus. I prayed for their hearts to remain soft and tender and not get hard, even when their worlds got hard. I prayed for Jesus to surround them with his love and light and that they would have a day that was filled with unexpected blessings. Each day, I craved this time. I pictured people in my head and pictured them surrounded by a loving white light. Not only did I know it was making a difference for them, but—wouldn't you know?—it was making a huge difference for me, too.

I felt my heart expand each time I prayed. I felt any unforgiveness or jealousy melting away. For those who I found hard to love, I cultivated immense compassion instead. It was a beautiful practice, and something that I will take with me with the rest of my life. The simple, yet pure act of praying for someone else is a gift for them, and for you. Give it a try.

Dear God,

Thank you for putting so many interesting people in our lives. We don't meet people by accident. Thank you for all of the beautiful lessons that they teach me every day. Please let me be a beacon of hope and love to everyone I encounter. May you work through me to be a blessing to others.

Amen.

LESSON TWELVE:

Flowers

The days after I got home from the hospital were filled with my doorbell ringing and the florist delivering endless numbers of beautiful bouquets from my beloved friends, coworkers, and family. Each one had an encouraging note letting me know that they were thinking of me, praying for me, and wishing me well in my recovery. I loved each of them. Each of them were different in their own ways—square vase, round vase, short vase, tall and skinny vase—mixes of purple, pink, yellow, and white perky flowers all perfectly arranged. My house was filled with the smell of the fragrant flowers and I breathed that in deeply.

One of the last arrangements that arrived was a small bouquet of white lilies that were still tight and un-bloomed. I admit, they were a little underwhelming compared to the other bright, gorgeous arrangements that I had received that were in full bloom. I put the lilies in water and waited that day, but they didn't bloom. The next day, I put them out on my deck to get a little sun. I'd anxiously peek out on the deck to see, but to my disappointment they still hadn't bloomed. I talked lovingly to the flowers, willing them to bloom.

Still nothing. My natural reaction was to not wait patiently for the flowers to bloom, but rather, I wondered, what if I helped a bit by prying one apart. Maybe it just needed a little coxing to bloom. On my deck, I took one of the lilies and gently began to pull open the tight pedals. They limply hung. It looked even worse than had I let it stay tight in its original state. Annoyed, I left the rest of the lilies in the vase and figured they were a dud batch. Days went by, and occasionally I'd look out of the window to my deck to see they still hadn't bloomed.

Then, one day, about a week later, they did. They opened so beautifully and fully. They smelled sweet and perfume-y. They were gorgeous. The one that I had pulled apart was the only exception. It was still limp and lifeless. In my hurry for it to bloom, I had ruined the surprise of it blooming in its perfect time. My eagerness took away its beauty.

And isn't it the same with life? When we try too hard to force—to push—to get to the outcome too quickly, it ruins the surprise. The flower doesn't bloom as it intended and often, instead, it withers and dies. Had I waited—just one week—the flower would have bloomed just as it was meant to. It wasn't late. It was perfectly on time. Our lives are the same. There is no need to push, to force, to chase, to demand the outcome that we see as best at the moment we want it. We wait on God's perfect timing. He knows best.

Dear God,

Thank you for teaching me the important lesson of waiting on your perfect timing. Often, I am in a rush. I want it all and I want it now. Teach me to slow down. Teach me to trust you.

Help me to know that at the perfect time, you will cause the right situations to bloom, and they'll turn out even more beautiful than we could have thought.

Amen.

LESSON THIRTEEN:
A Stupid Thing to Do

I was getting close to home from one of the hundreds of walks I took during the seventy days in the neck brace, when a woman who was also out on a walk spotted me and asked me what had happened.

"Sadly, I broke my neck," I replied, expecting her to meet my injury with compassion and tenderness.

"Well, that was a stupid thing for you to do. That was really stupid of you. I've never met anyone who has broken their neck. That was really, really stupid of you," she replied, shaking her head in surprise and disgust.

I simply replied, "Accidents happen," then forced a small smile and walked away. I was shocked. My mouth hung open in shock at what I had just heard. Stupid? How could she call me stupid? She didn't even know the circumstances behind what happened. What if someone had pushed me? What if I was a victim of a car accident? She had no idea. *How dare she!* I thought to myself. Then it hit me. In the back of my mind, I had been thinking I was stupid for falling down the stairs while not holding on to the handrail. Her comments to me were like a mirror, showing me the way I talk to myself, showing me how mean spirited it was to even think that I was stupid for making a mistake. And when I had been confronted with that fear face-to-face, I realized it was silly. I would never judge anyone for falling down the stairs, so why was I blaming myself and calling myself stupid?

I once read somewhere that we think around 60,000 thoughts each day, and of those, about 90 percent are negative about ourselves. If you had someone speaking more than 50,000 mean-spirited things to you each day, would you want to be around them? I didn't even want to be around that woman after one negative comment! So why are we doing this to ourselves?

I was thankful for the lesson that the woman that day taught me. I will not speak to myself any longer in a way that I would not speak to a stranger. I would never name call a stranger, therefore I will not name call myself. It's a daily practice. But, each day, I combat one more of those negative thoughts and replace it with compassion, just like I would when talking to a dear friend. Be careful what you tell yourself, you're listening.

Dear God,

Thank you for the lesson that the woman on my walk taught me. Thank you for letting me see how silly it was to call myself a name for making a mistake. Help me to remember I am your daughter. I am created in your perfect image. I am not perfect, but I am worthy of being talked to in a caring, loving, and thoughtful manner. Help me to talk to myself with the same compassion, kindness, and understanding that I give to others.

Amen

LESSON FOURTEEN:

Integrity

"You cannot drive until the neck brace comes off, at least eight weeks," my doctor told me plainly after my first appointment with her. I felt like I had the wind knocked out of me. *At least eight weeks without driving? No way! Didn't she know I was always in a rush for everything? That I was incredibly time conscious? That I would always choose the fastest way to get something done? I had finished my undergraduate degree in three years and my MBA in eleven months. Surely there was an accelerated path for healing, too, right?* I naively was expecting to be able to take the brace off and walk out of her office, since I was pain free and it has already been, in my mind, a whopping nine days of wearing it. Eight weeks of staying within the radius where my legs could carry me with a walk, or where an Uber would drive me? I felt panicked at the thought. I was used to my independence. I was used to getting up and going for any little thing.

"What if I just drive to work?" I negotiated. I couldn't help myself. "It's only a mile and half, it's a straight shot, and I'll go early and stay late if I need to in order to completely avoid traffic!" I tried my best to reason with the doctor.

"No," she replied. "No driving at all. You can't turn your head. You lack major visibility. It's simply not safe for you or for anyone else."

As soon as she walked out of the room, I leaned over to my mom who drove me to my appointment. "I think I can drive just a little, right?"

My mom smiled at me, knowing both me and my personality, and gently shook her head, compassion in her eyes.

This was going to be a real challenge for me. Would I follow the doctor's instructions or would I cheat when I felt like it, or when it was more convenient for me, without anyone being the wiser?

Maybe this was a test. A test to see if I would listen to instructions, even if I found them very limiting and highly inconvenient. A test to see if I would be able to look my doctor in the eye at the end of the eight weeks and honestly tell her I heeded her instructions and did what she recommended. Although annoyed at times, I'm proud to say I persevered. I'm able to look at my doctor and tell her I made it. I followed her instructions. I valued her medical opinion and the safety of myself and others more than the inconveniences that I suffered as a result of not driving.

The lesson in this? Integrity. I want to be known as someone whose words match their actions, someone who does the right thing even when they think no one is watching, someone who can be trusted for being sincere, even when you don't exactly see the point of it in the moment. And really, who doesn't want to be full of integrity? With God by my side, I was able to run and not grow weary, walk and not grow faint.

Dear God,

Thank you for giving me the heart to strive for integrity. Although I often fall short, I appreciate getting opportunities for my words to match my actions. Thank you for helping guide me through on days when I wanted to give up. I know, with you by my side, I can do all things.

Amen.

LESSON FIFTEEN:
Walking to Work

I used to say, "If I never had to drive a day in my life again, I'd be perfectly okay with that." Then, when I couldn't drive, I quickly realized how much I missed it and how convenient it was to have a car and the ability to drive anywhere I wanted to go whenever I wanted to go. I never equated driving with freedom until driving was taken away from me for seventy days.

I was grateful to live close to work. My townhouse was only one and a half miles, exactly, door to door from my office. I decided that while I was in my neck brace and unable to drive, I could get my steps in and walk to work. The doctor had given me strict orders that I was not to carry more than five pounds. The night before I walked to work the first day, I cleaned out my laptop bag, taking out everything but the absolute essentials. In the end, all that remained was my small work laptop, a pair of shoes to change into when I got to work, a piece of fruit for my snack (okay, okay, and a big piece of chocolate for after lunch), and my favorite lip gloss. All in all, this weighed in at five pounds.

The first morning that I walked to work, the weather was absolutely perfect. It was the beginning of July, bright and sunny at 6:30 a.m., a cool breeze, and seventy-one degrees. Ideal! As I walked, I listened to a podcast. Sometimes Joel Osteen, sometimes Joyce Meyer, sometimes a podcast I've grown to love called "7 Good Minutes." I would listen as I made the walk straight down Richmond road to Eaton Corporation.

Throughout all the weeks I walked to Eaton, it was perfect nearly every day. The same beautiful weather. The same cool breeze. What provision! If you know Cleveland, you know we aren't known for our stellar sunshine and weather. But, of all the days I walked, I only got lightly sprinkled on one day. Just one! Another God wink. Another way that God provided for me while I healed.

Dear God,

Thank you for the God-winks you show us. Thank you for the small and big ways that you show us your love and grace. Your provision always makes me smile. Thank you.

Amen.

LESSON SIXTEEN:
Surrender

Almost two weeks after my fall down the stairs, I began to get antsy. I was used to being on the go all the time. Now, my days were much quieter, and I had more time for stillness. At first, I wanted to fight this urge. I wanted to keep the same pace as I had before. I wanted to go to church in person. I wanted to meet friends for shopping and lunch. I craved going to hear live music and attend outdoor concerts. I wanted to work out. I so badly wanted back the normal life that I had. I had to surrender.

To me, surrender had always been synonymous with defeat. Giving up. Succumbing. Words that I didn't want to describe me or anything that I was involved in. I was a do-er. I like action. I like to push through.

But then I really thought about it. I changed my definition of surrender from giving up to accepting. Accepting that the moment I was in was important. Accepting that I wouldn't be in this place forever. Accepting that although I was getting used to my new normal, the new normal really wasn't bad, it was just different. Accepting that it could have been so much worse and that really I was blessed to be able to largely live normally during this time. The surrender turned to acceptance. The acceptance turned to gratitude. And, eventually, the gratitude turned to peace.

When I made that shift, it felt like a weight had been lifted off my shoulders. I was no longer fighting where I was. I was embracing that this short layover would teach me lessons and normal life would soon resume.

Dear God,

Surrender isn't easy. Thank you for teaching me that surrender doesn't mean succumbing. It means taking what I cannot control and putting it into your powerful hands. It's in no safer place. Please help me to continue to turn my upsets into surrender, surrender into acceptance, acceptance into gratitude, and gratitude into peace.

Amen.

LESSON SEVENTEEN:
Angel in the Woods

About halfway through my healing journey, I woke up one morning just feeling sad and inconsolable. Fear consumed me. *What if I never heal from this? What if I have to worry about this injury for the rest of my life and live incredibly carefully from now on? What if I make a wrong move in the future—maybe pick up something wrong—causing a shift in my neck and I'm paralyzed? What if all this walking that I'm doing is causing more harm than good? I read that I should drink bone broth to promote healing. Is that something that actually works? Maybe I should pick some up at the store today.* These thoughts and questions flooded my mind. Hot tears streamed down my face. I paced around my house, but the fear was unrelenting.

I decided that I needed some air. I wanted to walk to my favorite park, just more that two and half miles away from my house. The park was normally completely empty. Rarely did I run into anyone when I was there. I thought the alone time, cool breeze, and the light sunshine may give me a good release to think through these fears swirling through my mind. I put on my tennis shoes, left my house, and carefully made my way on the sidewalk down the long road until I reached the park entrance. As soon as I got into the woods, I broke down into sobs. I walked and sobbed. Suddenly, out of the corner of my eye, I saw someone in the distance. She was walking a large dog and waved at me. *What are the chances?* I thought, feeling annoyed. I had only run into a handful of people in the entire three years I walked in this park. I frantically wiped the tears away from my face and scrambled to find the sunglasses I had in my bag, and put them on in an attempt to hide my eyes, swollen and red from the crying.

"Good morning," I said quietly, hoping that she'd quickly say it back and I could keep walking and be alone again in my sadness.

"Good morning! Oh my gosh, you broke your neck, didn't you?" she asked.

"Yes, I fell down my stairs a few weeks ago," I said, trying to muster a small smile.

"Awww— I broke my neck fifteen years ago. I know what you must be going through. You're probably wondering if you're going to have to worry about this for the rest of your life. You're probably worried that one wrong move in the future and you could be reinjured, right? I had so much fear! The good news is that when you heal, your life will completely go back to normal. You won't even think about this a few months from now, I promise. And I love that you're walking. Walking several miles a day is the best remedy for broken neck. It helps to build bone density and helps with blood flow. You're doing the right thing. Until I saw you, I hadn't thought about my neck in many, many years. I've honestly never felt better in my entire life. I feel strong, and you will, too, I promise. Hang in there, okay? You're going to be stronger than ever soon! Don't worry! I recommend having some bone broth when you get home, too. So healing!" She smiled, and gave me a delicate hug. "And I love your neck brace! They've gotten much more fashionable over the years. You look great," she said and continued on her walk.

I stood there in stunned silence. Every fear and question I had in my head that I hadn't verbalized to anyone, she perfectly answered with affirmation and love. Every intricacy of my fear she addressed with optimism. She even mentioned bone broth! She told me I was doing the right thing. My tears returned, but this time they were happy tears.

I lifted my eyes up toward the sky and whispered, "Thank you," to God. Thank you for sending that woman to give me comfort and hope when I needed it the most. Thank you that she spoke from experience and squashed every fear that I had in my mind. Thank you that when I normally run into no one at this park, I ran into the perfect person who would give me peace and hope.

I walked at the park about twenty times in the following months of my healing. I didn't run into anyone else that entire time, and I haven't seen the woman who I talked to since. Earth angels are among us. I'm grateful that I got to experience mine on that day.

Dear God,

Thank you for sending earth angels to us in our darkest hours to fill us with hope and light. Let me be an earth angel to someone in the future, in their darkest hour.

Amen.

LESSON EIGHTEEN:
Blessed with Friends

I am so incredibly blessed with amazing friends. I knew that before my fall, but after the fall I realized with a fresh set of eyes how truly blessed I am. From a stream of texts wishing me well and asking what they could do for me while I was at the hospital, to being greeted with several bouquets of flowers and gifts when I arrived home, to picking me up to take me out to dinner during my recovery, to praying with me over the phone and offering to help in any way that they could, my friends went above and beyond for me.

One of my favorite quotes from from Jess C. Scott says, "Friends are the family you choose with your heart." My friends rallied around me for all seventy days of my healing, making me feel loved, appreciated, and well taken care of. I will never forget all that they did for me and can only hope that I can show them the same love, kindness, and loyalty that they showed me.

Dear God,

Thank you for the amazing gift of friendship, and the loving souls that you put on my path have filled me with such joy, hope, and happiness throughout my entire life. I am beyond grateful.

Amen.

LESSON NINETEEN:
The Lesson of Ivana Trump

During my recovery, I got an Apple news alert on my iPhone that read "Ivana Trump, Dead at 73." Clicking on the link to read through the news story about the life and untimely death of this well-known woman, I was fully expecting to see that she had passed away from a lingering illness kept out of the public eye. As I scrolled through the story, I quickly found out what caused her death, and it stopped me in my tracks. A fall down the stairs in her own townhome. I stood there in a stunned silence reading and re-reading the story over and over again. She had passed away from the very thing that I had survived just days before. My heart sank. "I'm so sorry, Ivana," I whispered under my breath, knowing the fear and pain she must have endured as she laid on her stairs, helpless, and took her last breaths.

Why did I survive and she didn't? I wondered.

This, too, was another lesson. The lesson of how precious and fragile this life really is. The lesson of reminding myself what if June 29, 2022, had been my last day? Would I have been ready? This thought made me sit in a quiet reflection.

Did my family know how dearly and truly I loved them? How I cherished them and how much joy they brought to my life? How I could be totally at peace and myself in their presence and how grateful I was for them?

Did my friends know how much it meant to me every time I saw their texts pop up on my phone? How it brought a smile to my face and how lucky I felt that our paths had crossed in this life? Did they know how much they added to my life? How I would play and replay memories of times that we had spent together over and over in my head and smile at the small details that made our time together so special? Did I ever fully express that to them?

Did my ex-husband and ex-boyfriends know that I have nothing but gratitude for the happy times together and complete peace and forgiveness for them and for myself for the times that they or I didn't act as our highest and best selves?

Did my pastors know how much I learned from them and how their words on Sundays always touched my heart and brought me closer to God?

Did my coworkers know that they make my job a total joy? That I love seeing them every day and that chatting by the kitchenette or in the salad bar line always meant so much to me?

Did the waiter at my favorite restaurant, cashier at my favorite grocery store, stylists at my favorite clothing store, and strangers that I saw around town know how much their kindness, smiles, and silly banter held a special place in my heart and that I treasured the brief, informal connections and interactions with them?

All of these thoughts swirled through my head. Thankfully, June 29, 2022, wasn't my last day on earth, but it was a day that has caused me to reexamine who I am and what is important to me, and has helped me gain clarity on leading a life with a legacy that I would be proud of.

What are those small things that you've put off saying to someone? Do they know how much you love them? How much you appreciate them? Is there something that you want to change in your life before it's too late?

Dear God,

Thank you for the gift of clarity. Thank you giving me a second chance to examine my life, my relationships and what brings me joy. Thank you for giving me the bravery to express my love and gratitude to those on the journey with me. Help me to leave a legacy of love.

Amen.

LESSON TWENTY:
The Hardware Store Angel

About a week after my encounter with the woman in the woods, another earth angel was sent to me. My mom came over every Saturday to help me clean and run errands. One particular Saturday, we discovered that I needed to get a spare key for my house made. I found the nearest hardware store online, and my mom drove me there to get the key made. When we arrived, there was a handwritten sign on the door saying the shopkeeper had to step out, and would be back in a few hours.

"Let's try another store," my mom suggested. Again, I found another hardware store online, this one a few miles way. The GPS successfully navigated us to a store that was off the beaten track a bit, an area that felt a bit rundown and unsafe. There was a light-up key on the window of the hardware store. "Look, they do make keys. Let's just run inside quickly and then we can get out of here," I said.

My mom and I walked through the parking lot into the store. The minute we opened the door, a beautiful cashier called out "Baby girl! Oh no! You broke your neck!" She promptly turned around, pulled up her ponytail, and revealed a large scar on the back of her neck. "I broke my neck, too, about five years ago. I remember wearing a neck brace just like the one you have on. Don't worry, baby girl, God is watching over you. You're going to heal. You're going to be perfect!"

The biggest smile came over my face. Again, what are the chances? I hadn't been in a hardware store in at least five years. The store we stopped in wasn't our first choice, and our judgements made us a bit hesitant to even step inside. But God once again gave me affirmation from an unlikely source. I thanked her profusely, got the key made, and we went on our way. On the way out, the cashier smiled and waved enthusiastically with the biggest smile. I will never forget this encounter, and the kindness, the sweetness, and the honesty that I was greeted with.

Dear God,

Thank you again for sending your love and messages to us, sometimes in unlikely places. I'm sorry for the times I judge unfairly. Thank you for still blessing me even when I'm hesitant.

Amen.

LESSON TWENTY-ONE:
Delay Does Not Mean Denial

Four weeks after the accident, I had a follow-up appointment with my doctor. I went in feeling good. I hadn't had any pain. I had been following her instructions to a tee: wearing my neck brace constantly without taking it off, not lifting anything weighing more than five pounds, and refraining from any exercise outside of walking. I was absolutely convinced that my good behavior was going to be rewarded with an accelerated timeline on my healing. First stop was the x-rays. I had to leave my neck brace on as they took x-rays from multiple angles of my neck and spine. Feeling confident that everything was healed, I then went down the hall to meet with my doctor. I was convinced that I would be neck-brace free in just a couple of weeks.

A couple weeks earlier, my friend Suzy asked me if I wanted to go on a beach vacation with her over Labor Day. If all went according to the original plan, my neck brace would be off by then, and I figured that would be the perfect way to celebrate my healing. I had accepted, but told her I would wait to book my ticket until after this appointment to ensure I would be cleared to travel by then.

I went in with a big smile to talk to the doctor. I excitedly told her how good I was feeling, how I was pain-free, and how I was pretty sure I was fully healed.

She smiled politely back at me, pulling up the x-ray on a bright screen in her office. "Everything is looking good and stable," she explained. "However, where your fracture is, is a very, very delicate part of the neck. I want to ensure it is fully healed before you can take the neck brace off. Because of that, I think we should add two more weeks on to my original estimate. That will put us at September sixth, the day after Labor Day."

"Are you sure? I feel great. I don't think I need the extra time. I've been wearing my brace 100 percent of the time, just as instructed." I could feel the urgency and panic in my voice.

"You're doing great. But, remember, you have a fracture in your neck. I don't want to take any chances. You need those extra weeks to ensure 100 percent healing."

I thanked her and agreed to her timeline.

As soon as I stepped out of the office, I began to cry. Hard. The disappointment in having the timeline extended by a couple of weeks seemed like a lifetime. I wouldn't be able to go on the trip with my friend Suzy. I would have to continue to walk anywhere I wanted to go for two additional weeks.

I got home, feeling sorry for myself, and cried some more. I pulled myself together enough to throw on some make-up. Suzy was coming over to take me to dinner. I let her know about the extended timeline, fighting back tears again, and letting her know I wouldn't be able to travel with her after all. She met me with compassion and complete understanding. Giving me a hug and reassuring me that we'd travel together one day soon, we went to dinner and caught up on life.

I had heard a quote months before that, and it bubbled up in the moment. "Delay does not mean denial." Just because my timeline was extended didn't mean that I wasn't healing. I repeated that quote to myself over and over and over again until it started to sink in.

Dear God,

Thank you for the reminders that delays do not mean denial. Your plans are for good, not harm. Help me to remember you see all the pieces while I see only a small fraction. Your timing is always the best. Your ways are always the best.

Amen.

LESSON TWENTY-TWO:

Message in the Rocks

During the pandemic, I used to walk at a park near my house. In March of 2020, one day, being bored with not seeing people, I wrote out the word "Hi" with a small pile of rocks on the path. The next day when I walked, I noticed the word had changed to "Hello." Smiling, I then changed the word to "Joy" and the next day was greeted with the word "Love" spelled out. This went on day after day for more than 300 days! In 2021, I finally met the lovely couple who was spelling out the words. It made me smile.

After my accident, on the weekends that my mom would come to help me with my grocery shopping, I'd always ask her if we could stop at the park quickly to do a small walk around the beautiful meadow where the rocks were. Every weekend she obliged, and we walked slowly together around the quarter-of-a-mile loop. At the end of the loop, there were the rocks that always spelled out a message.

"Awww!" I said to my mom, "Look, the rocks spell out heal!" I smiled and thought how nice it was to receive this special message.

"Wait, Ali, look!" my mom said, pointing, her mouth drawn down in disbelief, "It says, 'Heal Ali'!"

Sure enough, upon closer inspection, the word Ali was there, too.

The people who I had met the previous year had no idea I was injured. I snapped a picture and smiled at the divine message. I was healing and people were wishing me healing who didn't even know what was going on.

Dear God,

Wow! Thank you for kindness of strangers and for the prayers of others that we may not even know about. It is such a blessing to be surrounded by love. What a blessing.

Amen.

LESSON TWENTY-THREE:

Shannon's Blog

My talented friend Shannon is an accomplished health coach and yoga teacher. Over the years, she has developed a well-deserved following and writes a blog that she sends to her e-mail subscribers every couple of weeks. Shannon and I grew up two houses down from each other and have been friends our entire lives. We used to jump endlessly on the trampoline in our middle school days, and she was my travel buddy who invited me to go to Peru with her, on the trip that I had just returned from before my fall. Although we had been life-long friends, Shannon and I grew even closer on the trip. We took in the beauty of our surroundings, and we talked about our families and our relationships, about prayer and about God, and everything in between.

The night I fell, Shannon was one of the first people that I reached out to. I texted her asking her for prayers. I told her that I knew I was going to be okay, but I was very scared and sad that the fall and resulting injuries had happened. She soon texted me back and let me know she was praying for me. Throughout my recovery, Shannon texted me a few times a week to check in, came to my house to pick me up and take me on hikes and out for dinner, and let me know how deeply I was cared for.

About halfway through my recovery, Shannon called me one day and asked if I would be okay with her writing about me, my accident, my prayers, and my recovery in her latest blog. I was blown away. "Of course!" I replied and thanked her for the opportunity to share my story with her following.

Shannon wrote a beautiful blog about affirmative prayer and how well I had been healing. This was such a blessing. God has a funny way of turning things into his blessing and honor. In my healing, through a deep friend, I got to share a witness about God's love and healing in my life. How cool is that?!?

Dear God,

Thank you for turning messes into messages. Thank you giving beauty for ashes. Thank you for the opportunity to share about the power of prayer in the most unexpected way.

Amen.

LESSON TWENTY-FOUR:

Spirit Animal Clementine

Walking around my neighborhood one day, while wearing my neck brace, I ran into my beautiful neighbor Lauren and her adorable French bulldog, Clementine. Clementine is the neighborhood's friendliest dog and always brings a smile to the face of everyone that runs into her on her daily multiple walks.

Clementine and I have a lot in common. She, too, had a spinal fusion surgery and sports a long scar the length of her back. I had to smile brightly when I saw her that day. Why? Because not only was her scar showing but she was also wearing a cone around her neck, like the neck brace I was wearing! Turns out, Clementine had to have a medical procedure that week and had to keep the cone on twenty-four hours a day, seven days a week for it to heal. We were practically twins.

The funny thing is, Clementine didn't lose the pep in her step. She was happily walking around, sniffing like she normally did, and came right up to me to be pet. She hadn't lost her joy.

If Clementine could overcome this hardship, so could I! She, after all, is my spirit animal.

Dear God,

Thank you for making me smile continually. Thank you for the prefect reminders to still enjoy life, even in the midst of healing.

Amen.

LESSON TWENTY-FIVE:
They Had Little, Yet Were Generous With Me

Volunteering is a big part of my life. One of my spiritual gifts is having a soft heart toward people and helping people who are in need. It brings me so much joy to get to know people and their stories. I have been volunteering at my church, Mentor United Methodist Church, with a ministry called "More than a Meal" for about five years. On the last Saturday of each month, a group of volunteers from the church make meals that we pass out, drive-through style, to those who need a hot meal. I have loved getting to know everyone who comes to receive a meal. They are spirited, loving, and are always so grateful for this ministry. I get to play waitress, go and talk to each car, let them know what the dinner is, ask them if they have any prayer requests, and let them know that they are special and loved. One of my favorites that comes to More than a Meal is Elizabeth. Elizabeth is beautiful, has a heart of gold, and is an immigrant from Peru. I liked her from the minute I met her. She was smiling brightly and is always warm and caring. We've developed a friendship over the years.

I had texted her asking for prayers after my fall. She immediately responded to say how sorry she was for the accident and to let me know that she and her family were praying for me.

A couple of days later, a package showed up at my door. I delicately opened it to find a beautiful Peruvian jewelry holder with a nice note letting me know I was loved and that I was being prayed for. It was from Elizabeth.

I loved the gift, but knowing it was from Elizabeth made it even more special. She didn't have a lot, and yet she was generous with me. She got me a special gift, took time and money to mail it to me, and encouraged me in my healing. This was such a blessing and something that still gives me teary eyes when I think about it. It reminds me of the Bible story where the widow gives her last coin to the offering at the temple. She gave all she had. To me, that is so beautiful.

Dear God,

Thank you for putting people in my life who show me love and grace and give generously with an open heart. This means so much to me. I want to be like them. Help me to be generous with my love and grace to all I encounter.

Amen.

LESSON TWENTY-SIX:

Ripple Effect

One of my favorite quotes comes from Kurt Vonnegut, Jr. and says, "Don't let the world make you hard. Don't let pain make you hate. Don't let bitterness steal your sweetness. Take pride in the fact that although the rest of the world may disagree, you still find it to be a beautiful place."

One evening after work, I walked from my townhouse to the local grocery store. I grabbed a cart and placed in it a couple of items that I needed for the week that I forgotten to pick up when my mom had taken me grocery shopping over the weekend. I slowly pushed the cart up and down the aisles, making sure I wasn't forgetting anything else before I headed to the cashier to pay. The cashier checked me out and placed my items in one bag and handed it to me. I took the bag, said "Thank you" with a smile, and started to push my cart toward the exit door.

A lady suddenly appeared next to me and insisted, "Let me take your cart for you, please."

"No, that's okay," I said, not wanting to be an inconvenience.

"Please, let me take your cart. I will return it for you. I broke my neck a few years ago and remember wearing a brace like yours. At that time, I remember someone at the store offering to help me, and I remember how good it felt. Let me help you, please."

I smiled, thanked her, and told her how much I appreciated her paying it forward by doing something good for me. I promised that I would one day return the favor to someone I saw in a neck brace , to keep her random act of kindness going.

This lady made my day. I love that she had gone through the same thing years earlier, remembered the kindness of a stranger, and had passed it on. I loved that she shared her story with me. I love that she didn't take no for an answer and inspired me to be on the lookout for ways that I could help others in the future.

Although the world isn't always good, there is always good in the world. I loved that reminder.

Dear God,

Thank you for the people you put in our paths. Thank you for strangers offering to help us on our journeys. Thank you for the ripple effect of kindness. Please allow me to pass this on by being a blessing to someone in the future who needs love, compassion and to be seen in the moment that they're in.

Amen.

LESSON TWENTY-SEVEN:
God Never Blinks

My friends had been so generous with me throughout my entire recovery—dropping off gifts, sending texts, picking me up and taking me places—it was all so nice. My friend Shannon had given me a book that she had come across called *God Never Blinks*. This beautiful book is a collection of short stories of God's goodness from a cancer survivor. Each story was full of hope and made me smile. I had been reading one short story a day.

One night I was sitting out on my balcony patio reading the book, and I noticed how perfect it was outside. A smile came to my face. It was a warm and muggy evening in July. It was the perfect temperature to sit outside and soak up the peak of the summer. That night, the chapter turned out to be about a boy who was doing a flip on the trampoline when he landed wrong and, of all things, ended up breaking his neck.

"Can you live if you've broken your neck?" the little boy in the book asked after realizing that he was now paralyzed from the neck down and would never walk again. As soon as I read it, I quickly set the book down. Tears streamed down my cheeks.

I sat in silence for a few minutes, trying to grasp that reality. That could have been me. Instead of being outside, noticing the perfect temperature and casually flipping through my book, I could have been paralyzed. I could still be in the hospital. I could be living in a full-time rehab center for the rest of my life.

Instead, I was safe. I was in my beautiful townhome. I was pain free. I was calm and relaxed, reading outside. A flood of gratitude washed over me. Moments before, what I was doing seemed pretty ordinary and, quite frankly, boring. But, in this moment I realized, the little things in life are truly the big things in life. The boring and ordinary moments are the exact moments that are most beautiful to be alive. That book was the perfect reminder not to take anything for granted. Simply being able to walk outside and hold my book on my own was the perfect reminder of how truly blessed I was. It's true, God never blinks.

Dear God,

Thank you for the moments of realization that I experienced on my road to recovery. Thank you for opening my eyes to being able to see that the ordinary moments of life are so precious—and such a miracle.

Amen.

LESSON TWENTY-EIGHT:

Twenty-Twenty-Twenty-Four Hours to Go!

Labor Day was the day before my doctor's appointment that would determine if I was healed enough to be able to take off the neck brace and slowly begin to resume my normal activities, like driving and easing back into workouts. My mom came and picked me up at my house to drive me back to my parent's house where they would have a cookout later in the day. When we arrived at my parent's house, a rush of excitement rolled through me.

"Just think," I said to my mom "this time tomorrow, I may be able to drive again!" I said excitedly. To celebrate the countdown, I pulled up the song "I Wanna Be Sedated," by the Ramones. As the song played on my phone, my mom and I danced around the kitchen singing along with the lyrics, "Twenty-twenty, twenty-four hours to go- oh- oh"

I was so excited. It felt like I had been running a marathon and the finish line was now within sight. The end was near. The perseverance had paid off and I would soon know if I would be healed. I couldn't wait. The whole cookout, I had excited butterflies in my stomach. I was going through a list of all of the things that I would do as soon as I could drive again. Mitchell's Ice Cream was the first on my list. Anticipation filled every ounce of my spirit. I love that feeling!

Dear God,

Thank you for the feeling of anticipation, of waiting to see what you are going to do and how you are going to move. It's exciting. It lights up my soul. Let my eyes stay wide to all the ways you continue to work around me and within me daily.

Amen.

LESSON TWENTY-NINE:
Healed

Seventy days after my fall, I had my follow-up doctor's appointment to check on my healing and to see if I could discontinue wearing the neck brace. That morning, I woke up with giddy anticipation that it was over and life would soon return to normal, but it was mixed with a pit in my stomach wondering if I would require more time to heal and have to continue with my treatment. As I put on my tennis shoes and grabbed my laptop bag to walk to work, I opened the door to my condo and was greeted by a heavy fog and rain. To me, this wasn't a good sign. This was the first day that it had rained in the morning and would require me to walk with an umbrella on my way to work. "This may be the last time you have to do this," I reminded myself as I stepped back inside, grabbed my oversized umbrella, and tucked my hair into my shirt to avoid it getting ruined by the rain and fog. I made it about twenty steps before running into my neighbor, who was standing in her garage, leash in hand, as her dog happily pranced in the rain.

"You're not walking in this, are you?" she asked. "Can I give you a ride?" she sweetly asked.

The biggest smile came over my face. "Yes, yes, please if you have time?"

She gladly agreed, and a minute later, I was in the comfort of her dry car, being chauffeured down the road to work. I smiled at the sky again, "Thank you," I whispered. To me, this was another confirmation that God was watching over me and was protecting me over these past seventy days. My neighbor dropped me off and told me to text her after my appointment so we could celebrate the good news of getting my brace off. I thanked her, agreed to text her, and happily—and dryly—stepped into work.

The morning went quickly and, before I knew it, my mom was at my office to pick me up and take me to the doctor. The plan was to get x-rays first to check on the healing, followed by a meeting with my doctor where she could review the x-rays and make a call on the next steps for my treatment. My mom and I held hands when we arrived in the hospital parking lot, prayed and thanked God that I was healed, and that life as I formerly knew it would resume. I was able to get the x-rays quickly, and then off to the waiting room we went for my appointment.

After just a couple minutes of waiting, the doctor called us in. "I just reviewed your x-rays," she said happily. "You are completely healed. Everything looks great. You can take off your brace. It looks so good, that I don't think you even need physical therapy. I can give you a few exercises to do on your own at home. I mean in this in the nicest way possible, but I hope to never see you again. You are healed and healthy and won't have to worry about this ever again."

I quickly sprung out of my chair, took my neck brace off, gave my doctor and my mom the biggest hug, and whispered "Thank you, thank you, thank you" under my breath over and over again. This was more than I could have asked for. It was over. I was healed. No physical therapy. Wow. I was amazed and grateful. I slowly moved my head back and forth, up and down and in small circles. There was no pain. There was no stiffness. I felt completely normal, like it never happened. Just like the Earth angels in the woods and at the hardware store had promised me, it was over. My health was restored. I was beaming. I couldn't stop smiling. My mom and I stopped to hug at least five times on our way out of the hospital. I excitedly clapped my hands and cheered over and over again. Once outside, I lifted my arms up towards the sky and twirled around, squealing with excitement in the parking lot. When I got into my mom's car, I immediately pulled down the passenger-side mirror and examined what I looked like without my neck brace on. The whole drive home, I gently caressed my neck and continued to make small movements with it. As soon as my mom pulled into my development, I asked her "Do you want to go for a ride? My car? I'll drive!"

We laughed, and that's exactly what we did next.

Dear God,

Thank you so much for the gift of health and the gift of healing. So often, we take our health for granted, never noticing how good it is until it's temporarily gone. Thank you for restoring health back to me. Thank you for giving me more than I could think or imagine. Thank you, thank you, thank you.

Amen.

LESSON THIRTY:
Grateful for the Journey

It's now been six months since my fall. As I reflect back, it all feels like a blur. It happened quickly, the recovery was smooth, and my life resumed back to its normal busyness shortly after getting the brace off. Since that day, I have reflected many times on the journey and on the lessons I learned. The main lesson: gratitude. I'm grateful for healing. I'm grateful to be pain free. I'm grateful for all the kindness that I experienced on the way. I'm grateful to share my story. I'm grateful to have grown closer to God in the process. I'm grateful to be more mindful and I am grateful to be more appreciative of every-day moments.

The other day, I was at a doctor's appointment for my annual physical. The nurse was asking me about my medical history and was curious if anything had changed with me or my health in the past year. After hearing about my injuries, the nurse grabbed my arm and said, "Wow, you are really, really lucky. God must have a very important assignment for you to do still."

I smiled, and my heart burst with joy at hearing her words. I agree, and I can't wait to see what it is.

Dear God,

Thank you for this experience. I'm grateful for all I learned throughout this entire process. I'm grateful for total healing. I'm grateful you were by my side and remain by my side. I am grateful that You are God of the valleys and you are God of the mountain peaks. Life is quite an adventure – high highs and low lows. I'm here for it all. Thank you. I love you.

Amen.